Emotion Evoking People and Words Written With the Intent To Represent My Interactions With Aforementioned People

Emotion Evoking People and Words Written With the Intent To Represent My Interactions With Aforementioned People

William L. Howard

Tampa, Florida

The content associated with this book is the sole work and responsibility of the author. Gatekeeper Press had no involvement in the generation of this content.

Emotion Evoking People and Words Written With the Intent To Represent My Interactions With Aforementioned People

Published by Gatekeeper Press
7853 Gunn Hwy., Suite 209
Tampa, FL 33626
www.GatekeeperPress.com

Copyright © 2024 by William L. Howard
All rights reserved. Neither this book, nor any parts within it may be sold or reproduced in any form or by any electronic or mechanical means, including information storage and retrieval systems, without permission in writing from the author. The only exception is by a reviewer, who may quote short excerpts in a review.

Library of Congress Control Number: 2024940898

ISBN (hardcover): 9781662953279
ISBN (paperback): 9781662953262
eISBN: 9781662953286

DEDICATION

Dedicated, as always in all ways, to Lillie
(without You there is no Me)
and to the people who evoked the emotion of Love and
P.E.A.C.E. within me

*

Special dedication to
Linda
Who has been there for me and remains to be, steadfast and
unwavering, in the best and worst of my moments

FOREWORD
─────────

Upon reading this book of poetry, there may be certain individuals who might feel slighted or curious as to why they were not included, or omitted from my musings. As an explanation, I simply offer you this: The first of my creations was composed days short of my twenty-third birthday in June of 1994. A relatively recent acquaintance of mine introduced me (telephonically) to his girlfriend's cousin and she and I established communication relations through phone conversations. She was in a relationship that plagued her mentally, physically, and emotionally, yet she could not fathom being without him. She desired to leave, yet she stayed. She hated him, yet she loved him. She was beyond me; she was BLONDIE. Shortly thereafter, on August 10, 1994, the most magnificent monumental momentous event occurred. Blessed is the birth of a Beautiful child, and so it was written ... BRIANNA. Prior to both of those moments, on January 26, 1994, my beloved Mother died and her being the soul foundation of my very existence, you would have surmised, upon her demise, I would have written verses of unequivocal eloquence and elegance in deference to her essence, as she was no longer physically present. Well, my period of mourning was immensely extensive exceeding far beyond years, even drifting into decades. I have candidly told a few Family members, of which some already knew, and shared with DAMARIS, DAWN, and LYTE, and now I share with you, the reader. I figuratively and a little literally "lost my mind" when Eye lost Lillie. The night before she died, she was more focused and concerned about my safety and well-being than adhering to her own wellness. She had been ill, yet her death was definitely unexpected; For the Love and Light she radiated to any and everyone, fifty-one was far too young. Thus my emotions were overtly overwhelming and critically impacted my Life; hence it took me 7 years, 4 months, and 24 days later to write ... LILLIE (the 1st of 3, 4u2 see as you continue to read). The compositions written in this book were created some time ago, with the exception of KHAI. Although there are more Emotion-Evoking People I could certainly write about, I Am disinclined to do so, due to my declining interest in having to think more craftily and creatively than I care to lately. I will, however, acknowledge the following individuals, in no particular order, with the sentiment of P.E.A.C.E. Love & Respect. The "Flint Street Families"/ The Allen Family - Parents Michael Sr. and Maxine, Children Dawn, Erica, and Michael Jr. / The Brantley Family - Parents Dorace and Alice, Children Kenneth and Keith / The Clark Family - Parents Prince Sr. and Denetta(?)Dee, Children Onna, Prince Jr., and Brick / The Gause Family - Parents Robert Sr. and Carolyn, Children Barrick, Marie, Ray "Von," Robert Jr., and Andre / The Glasgow Family - Parents Herbert and Sumalee, Children Gerald, Marcus, and Damon / The "Plymouth Street" Greene Family - Parents Joe and Shirlette(?), Children Bridgette, Shandreta, John, and Gregory / The Haygood Family - Parents Neil and Gwen, Children James "Jimmy" and Corey / Allen and Emily Jenkins / The Jackson Family - Mother Betty, Children Roderick, Wanda, and Betty(?) / The "Seward Street" Jackson Family - Parents Jesse and (?), Children Timothy, Tyrone, and Todd / The Johnson Family - Parents Abe and Mary, Children Aaron, Gloria, John, Timothy, and Thomas / The Kelly Family - Mrs. Kelly, Children Missy, Noni, and Tracy / The "Plymouth Street" Kerr Family - Parents Renford Sr. and Sandra, Children Renford Jr. "Craig", Ozzie, Andrea, and Michelle / The Radcliff Family - Parents Francis and Rebecca, Children Regina, Christopher, Alexander, and Andrea / Shawn and Michael Wade / Sandra Solomon / Charles "Chuck" Fitzgerald / Arthur "X" Fitzgerald / Andre Waters / Tina Waters / Brenda Daniels / Krista Hudnell

/ Sherri Glen / Timothy McGowan / Terrance Holmes / Kenneth McFadden / James Barron / Don Swain / James "Jah" Elmore / Darnell "Suge" Williams / Patrice Hale Jr. / Damon Glasgow Jr. / Nicole McEwen / Ashley Lester / Elijah Malik Howard / Dorien Broady / Darian Broady / Mark Moore / Julio Vazquez / Leroy Vazquez / Deidre "Kali" and Maui / RahYin Quantum / Ienindra of the Nederlands / Gregory Chappelle / and last B.U.T. never the least, to my entire Howard Family relatives from, and currently residing in, Florida and Georgia.

Please Be Advised: Due to the fact that Eye do not have, nor ever had, any personal knowledge, affiliation, or relationship with any of the musical artists who Eye bestow P.E.A.C.E. Love & Respect upon in the upcoming pages, my acknowledgments are strictly for their musical abilities, creations, and contributions, of which the majority mentioned influenced me in positive and/or productive ways, specifically, but not limited to, from the mid 80s to the late 90s .

Wisdom with the absence of knowledge is wasted

I've heard that ignorance is bliss, but it may evolve to hatred

Love is an emotion we have yet learned to master

Love can be exquisite or it may lead to disaster

Idealistically we exist to be beings of extreme reverence

And to praise thee Almighty in Its Supreme benevolence

Much to my chagrin, Eye have yet to embrace Its Light

    But before this ode's end, I sincerely think Eye might.

Wisdom Once Revealed Located and Deciphered

Positive Energy Activates Continuous Enlightenment

Life without you leaves me lost and hopeless

I don't believe Eye even know anymore what hope is

Looking to the future, Eye can't seem to focus

Looking to make my pain disappear; hocus pocus

I went from living a Loving Life to a troubled life with no notice

Eventually Eye Will see The Light and get Right; Know this.

Life without You is unbearable to me

I've become someone quite terrible to be

Lustful and lawless, two of a few negative traits I've accquired; in

Life You were trustful and flawless, inspiring me to ever rise higher

In death You are martyred, partnered with angels of your ilk

Ever so Blessed am I to possess a Lillie that Will never wilt.

Laughter lasts only until the day before tomorrow

In mere moments after laughter, soon may come sorrow

Life is like many things, complex and unexplainable

Life without You is like reaching for the unattainable

If Eye should ever endeavor to ascertain the true meaning

Evidence would be prevalent, revealing You as a true pure Being.

LMH FOR LIFE / LMH4LYFE

Lillie Mae Howard "Eye" LoveYouForEver

Lately I've Lived Life Inexplicably Empty

because

Life without You is like a World without trees

I'm alive, yet often, it's difficult to breathe

Left with little breath, I desperately cling; to

Life as Eye know it, without knowing One thing

If I shall ever be Blessed to bask in Your Divinity; or

Eternally yearn to be thee Creator of Your soliloquy.

*

Where is daddy? Who is daddy? Why is daddy **SO** angry?

Is it my fault? That's what I thought. Daddy why not just blame me

Lillie tell me, why you ever let him beat You like that?

Life is too sacred to waste it; please Lillie, fight back

It took 24 years and many more tears for me to forgive you for your treachery

Even though you put Her through Hell, Eye know Heaven is where She's

    Blessed to be.

Strength was never an issue for you; you never seemed to be weak

Though you've endured losses in the game of Life, you've always
managed to compete

As a youth, in truth, I may have idolized you a bit too much

Now as a grown man myself, Eye respect you equally as such

Learning to rise higher from prior mistakes is what makes us mentally
stronger

Emotionally equipped and physically fit to exist in this game a bit longer

Yet our aim in this game is not to merely maintain on the same level,
or simply exist

At times we conflict in our points of interest,

but we both want to win at this shit.

Reflect in depth upon a time when death and utter chaos controlled us

And evil "Inner-G" was the only entity friendly enough to console us

Now envision a new beginning, a true extension of solidarity

Divinity is within me, within you too; Are you there with me?

Years shall pass in days, yet of those days that shall pass

    We will have no recollection, merely a reflection of our past.

    -AKA-

Wisdom of a Prophet

Actions at times opposite

Knowledge in abundance

Insanity can be encumbered

Madness or magnificence

    tragedy or beneficence

    tragically it's irrelevant

    because

    He was hellbent to be Heaven-sent.

Lately we, regrettably, haven't communicated that much

It's not uncommon; we have that in common; to drift in and out of touch

Nowadays, when passing ways, we may passively say a few words out of Love and Respect

Despite what others may deem indifference, that's just how we connect

Admittedly Eye can see some of Willie's features in me; and I shared with you how he stared through me in the mirror;

But then Eye looked to you and you spoke, and Linda, no joke,

Not only did Eye see Lillie in You; Eye could also hear her.

Thus what was once a momentary curse; dissipated, evaporated, dispersed, as if on cue

Due to the sheer fear of Lillie's Light that emanated from You.

Afraid to be perceived as less than a man

Lillie always believed in you, which we truly didn't understand

From our point of view you were simply another hand

Reaching for currency for an emergency or one of your plans

Eventually, we would come to agree, we didn't see you nearly enough

Death has an effect that makes you reflect on those you sincerely Love.

*

Remember when Eye initially set foot on Florida earth

It was you, my truest cousin, who Willie took me to see first; Eye

Couldn't bring myself to watch your health diminish slowly, yet Eye

Knew you'd understand, and that final look in your eyes told me

    That we'd smile and laugh again; another place, some other time

    Where your Southern Player mentality meets my New York State

    of Mind.

(Rest In Power "Slick" Rick Howard and Uncle Alfred Horne
- ICU both on the other side)

MENDACITY

Is my perception of our connection perceived accurately?
Have you crafted deception to perfection to deceive me masterfully?
Because my 3rd Eye vision functions actively
Allow me to enlighten you as to why I'm writing you so tactfully.
You see; your means and motivation for establishing communication
Was to receive information for the day of my emancipation
And my intended destination upon my release from incarceration;
Is that the general situation? Is there no venerable explanation?
Is there truth in this revelation? Is your emotional elevation in an extreme state of stagnation? I once was deep in contemplation, contemplating capitulation with thoughts of you as my salvation; now I'm faced with the realization that I've succumb to manipulation ... through ... MENDACITY.

(Menda - city)
Mendacity (noun) - tendency to lie; untruthful,
dishonest, deceitful

Mother of my offspring; my first true Love

Even when we were suffering together, we knew Love

Never did Eye ever intend to forsake you for another

Damn! As your man Eye even overlooked My Mother

And yet, here we are from Loving start to Unfulfilled finish

    Too many miles apart and two hearts greatly diminished.

Reality may be what we perceive it to be

Exceptions may be not believing in me

No amount of distortion can contort the proof

Even distractions don't detract from the Truth

Everything done in the dark comes to Light

    Whether by Candle-aria, no candelabra is right.

P.E.A.C.E. Love & Respect to Israel Deveaux,
Menda's Husband

Blessed is the birth of a Beautiful child

Raised by Mother Earth while Father Universe was exiled

Initially, she was to be our greatest Love unspoken

Alas, as time passed, our bond became broken

Now lies hide a hate, where there once was deep Love

No longer do we relate; no Love to speak of

At least not in the sense of how intense it used to be.

But

Realistically

Inexplicably

Since

Her

Entrance

To

This

Existence I've been insistent to reveal the real me; not just who you choose to see.

Keeping with tradition, the latest addition to my pedigree

Holds the distinguished distinction of being greater than Eye could ever be

Already, not incredibly, his Mother has surpassed my every expectation

In a sense, his innocence represents my reverie of Revelation

Knowledge sets me free

Apathy is the path for me

Mastered my mentality

Opaque in my morality

Reflective of my originality

Introspective of my objective

      To transcend dimensionality.

P.E.A.C.E. Love & Respect to Jakari,
Brianna's Husband and Khai's Father

During your Mother's pregnancy, we anxiously awaited your birth

Adding to our excitement was that you would be the first

Nephew or niece bequeathed to our Family

In a volatile environment you brought P.E.A.C.E. and tranquility

Everything about you led me to believe; the

Lord, Himself, enabled Linda to conceive

Looking back on those days of you as a baby, I knew by far

Eventually you would grow into the beautiful, successful Woman you are.

P.E.A.C.E. Love & Respect to Amir and Aubrianna,
Danielle's son and daughter

That sly mischievous grin that tends to warm the hearts of many; is

Exactly the happy-go-lucky look that causes some to envy

Very few youths in our community receive the blessings that you do

In truth, I trust you'll learn to believe and accept what Eye say is true

Navigate on a path so straight that crooked cease to exist

    Remain steadfast in your Natural state of Love and P.E.A.C.E.fulness.

*

Guess what World? You have a new niece

Amidst a pit of convicts, I've been blessed with true P.E.A.C.E.

Life's given a new lease to my sister and Eye

You've lifted our Spirits above any mountain high

News of this Nature is due cause for elation

    Commence the celebration to welcome the next generation.

P.E.A.C.E. Love & Respect to Kamayia and Alina,
Tevin's daughters

P.E.A.C.E. Love & Respect to Kayden,
Galyn's son

As Eye recall we first met in the direct center of the U.S.

Nearly ninety miles north of Wichita, in Junction City, Kansas

During my brief stay outside the base of Fort Riley, Eye

Recall your sweet face as you smiled ever so shyly

Elegance combined with a complete sense of self-worth

Now Eye understand why Stan faithfully placed you first

In his heart, soul, and Spirit; indeed in his mind

As for me, you'll forever be Family, a sister of mine.

*

Okay, in all honesty, I'll have to admit; Eye

Can't concentrate, but wait; I can't quit

Especially for someone so beautiful and bright

At times I'm at a loss; what to say, what to write; even

Now my mind wanders, my thought patterns scatter

Andrenia and you are two people in my Life who will always matter.

Jealously is an ugly burden I'm certain you'll have to carry

Others will envy you immensely for reasons that may vary

Some simply because you stand tall and majestic; yet

Harboring those sentiments make them small and pathetic

Amidst their ceaseless rumors, you shall rise above it

Until you've attained the higher ground and I'll look down and Love it; so

No matter the chatter, or topic of gossip for the moment

    Don't succumb to that dumb shit, march to the beat of your own

    drum kit, and never the beat of your opponent.

*

Madness tends to permeate the most magnificent minds

Add to the list this basically bonded bound blood brother of mine

Real genius, some insist, is inflicted with a hint of insanity; the

Kind of genius when extinguished designates you the Black Sheep

    of the Family.

P.E.A.C.E. Love & Respect to Ayanta, Calandria, & Bessie
(my Sisters & their mother)

Before we partook of our holy matrimony, Eye

Rightfully knew it would be You for Me only

Even before you agreed to be my wife,

Everything that really mattered, I already had in My Life.

> The Love of a GOoD Woman and 3 beautiful daughters
>
> A Love deeper than the depths of the deepest of waters
>
> A Love which was nourished by respect, honor, and truth
>
> And as our Love flourished, the man in me grew.

*

Beauty personified beyond all specifications

Reality surpasses the fantasy of my innermost expectations; the

Energy you radiate sates my innate inhibitions

Exactly as Eye thought it, you brought it to fruition.

> Bree was once my wife so Eye wrote about her twice. We built a
>
> Beautiful Life but Love did not suffice. We agreed to blame me, yet
>
> Eye let her remain blame-free, for the sake of A & T

T ogether we'll endeavor to overcome any obstacle

I n truth, we've achieved more than many believed possible

E ven when you were "beyond reproach" and no one dared to bother; Eye

R econstituted a different approach and became a Loving, caring Father

R esults were rendered gradually; we were glad to see you excel

A nd to this day, we're ecstatic to say, that all with you is well.

*

A re You the most perfect child GOD has designed?

M ay Eye take credit for developing your mind?

A re You indeed the seed planted One of a kind?

Y our aura emanates radiance, so brilliant as to blind

A midst an abyss of darkness, will You continue to shine?

P.E.A.C.E. Love & Respect to Aiyanna & Anthony,
Tierra's daughter & son

P.E.A.C.E. Love & Respect to Aniya & Peter,
Amaya's daughter & son

Kings preside over masses keeping their nations well protected

Either you were hated, Loved, or feared, but always well respected

Neighborhoods throughout the ROC were shocked by your

    untimely demise

Nothing is forever; thus the immortal man finally dies

Yet your name remains amongst us; your legacy etched in memory

Because many now call me Kenny and as they knew you, they too,

    will remember me.

*

Kind of hard being the younger baby brother of a Legend

Even when you headed in the right direction, you could dead end

If you followed in his footsteps you took steps to do it better

Traveled your own path; became a trendsetter

Honored your brother well, your Mother Alice, and yourself

Best of success, be ever Blessed and in the best of health.

J.

Life is quite real or is Life what you make it?

If I reveal how Eye really feel, how will you take it?

Given the condition of my metaphysical history

Happiness for me is a metaphysical mystery

Time has an unkind way of playing tricks with one's mind

Freedom is what we fought for, and finally Eye won mine

Open the passage of communication; unification made through One line

Our friendship eclipsed illumination, from '77 in the 1st grade,

    to our graduation of '89

Then we set up shop; made lots of plays; til '94 and went our separate ways

    Look how far we've come from those desperate days.

Memories we created exist through the many roads we traveled

As you proceeded to take a right in Life, I went left and unraveled

Ultimately our converging paths veered off in opposite directions

Resulting in the aftermath of a rash of biopic reflections

In all the towns we'd visit, we always found exquisite pieces; even in

Cleveland, GOD revealed to us what P.E.A.C.E. is

Except I made a misstep and ended up doing time

    But Moe, as you now know, I too, am doing fine.

J.

    -aka- Moe

Birds take to flight as day turns to night

Love turns to hate if the Love is not right

Over the years many tears have been cried

Not due to physical pain, but the pain from inside

Deep-rooted emotions we all partake of; especially

If you've ever experienced the feelings of Love

Everyone has a fate they must face in their Life

        But Love turns to hate if the Love is not right.

*

Majestic; like the Queen You were bred to be

And Me as your King, eternally

United as One, in our Kingdom of glory

Determinedly defending our never-ending terrority

Enrapt in the riches we so sacredly cherish

        That wealth being our Love, which without, we shall perish.

P.E.A.C.E. Love & Respect to Maude Ely, who figuratively & literally saved me from drowning, lifting me from the submerged depths of Keuka Lake in the summer of 1992

Throughout our years together, we explored every possible pleasure,
yet never a moment of pain

I'll never forget after my Mother's death, when Menda left,
how You kept Me somewhat sane

Selfless in every sense; completely uninhibited

Helpless, you gave me strength; your passion, pure, unlimited

Even though you had a home of your own to maintain; you

Kept providing me with stimulation for the activation of my brain

As lustful as we were together, there was also a shared bond of honor

Plus, you too, gave birth to a baby girl in August '94 and also aptly
named her Brianna.

Do you recall the Saint Paul waterfall?

Are you still built bodacious Amazonian tall?

Voluptuos Vixen

In the bedroom plus kitchen

Sensuous Temptress, my Princess, my Empress

Don't ever be afraid to engage me in my madness; but

Aren't you the princess Eye placed on a pedestal in my palace

We bared our souls in the snow; you were there when I lost control

Never knew the things I'd do would leave your heart with such a hole

*

Linked by the way we think and react under pressure

You kidnapped your first wife as a nice, Loving gesture; I

Took a bullet and put it through the leg of my first Love

Each of us committed atrocities we're not exactly proud of

    We are, indeed, kindred Spirits with genuinely kind souls

    Whether we find the P.E.A.C.E. that we seek, Eye suppose

    only GOD knows.

Lissandra was knock-kneed, pigeon-toed, and bow-legged

It might sound unappealing but her step kept me hard-headed

She walked wantonly without even trying; her

Stance entranced me hauntingly; Eye ain't even lying

At Genessee Valley Park Eye delved **DEEP** in her in the dark

Night after night we'd "playfight" and we'd leave our marks

Didn't hesitate when that cat let that massive gat explode

Running fast past my own home to reach the safety of her abode

And the comfort of her home became my comfort zone

>   Or as we casually called it; my come for her zone.

Before you, Eye knew only solitude and seclusion

Reveling in reveries which were merely illusions

Imagining my future to be as bleak as my past

Talking to myself, no one else would speak to my ass

Then you came along and what's wrong became right

At least Eye knew Peace and delved **DEEP** on that night

Next night the same; we came, together for eight days straight

You fed me your Afro-Cuban cuisine and I ate everything on my plate.

Very few ladies

In this Lifetime of mine

Could physically "drive me cray-z"

Essentially without even trying

Now, she had me madly in Lust like just 4 or 5 others

Twisted me into thinking my lust for her was Eye Love her

Even though she was the "Baddest Bitch," her words not mine;

    Eye agreed, decreed her "My Goddess"; she called herself

    "Sunshine."

My Goddess (Sunshine)

You know you're my Goddess and exactly what that means to me
You know that this Life is not My Life it's just a dream to me
You know My Creator made me greater than Eye seem to be
You know Eye don't play but if Life is a play this just One scene to me
You know Eye don't change just because Eye change my scenery
On any side of the fence Eye represent the grass is green to me
Even though my hands so dirty they will never come clean to me
Even though they may call you a hoe you will never not be a Queen to me.
—To Brittany Vicente

*

(The following does not pertain to Brittany Vicente. This Brittany (surname undisclosed) was cool to be with but chaotic when conflicted due to several diagnosed mental health issues she struggled with)

Beauty is often described yet never fully defined

Reality in actuality is perception of One's mind

Insanity and ingenious are merely genuses combined

The brain contains both but keeps the most harmful confined

Through the course of time, the threads may unravel or unwind

A Saint becomes a sinner when the center splits its mind

Now what was once Holy is wholly rendered in half

You seek to save your soul, yet fail to walk the rite path.

Born innocent; born in a sense, to bring joy to those around her

Once exposed to those who opposed her innocence, wickedness began
      to surround her

Beset upon by evil men, and women who weren't much better

Believing her only outlet was about death, she tried but GOD wouldn't let her

I have so much more in store for you, dear sweet child of mine

Even in the darkest of times, your light shall surely shine.

Knowing who and what you are and knowing your true worth

Is what molds you and shapes you to make you Mother of this Earth

Now knowing that you are the very essence of the image of which you
      were made in

Give thanks and praise for the Blessing you received, which we believe
      is Jayden.

CAUTION: Extremely intelligent Black man instilling hope in the Black community

HAZARDOUS: Can this new age *"Prophet Of Rage"* invoke the hope of Black unity?

URGENT: There's *"Muse Sick-n-Hour Mess Age"*; if you listen you will learn

CHAOS: Catastrophic events are imminent when we *"Burn, Hollywood, Burn"*

KING's legacy wasn't honored, so *"By The Time I Get To Arizona"*; in fact

DANGER: They'll brand Chuck *"Public Enemy #1"* because *"It Takes A Nation Of Millions To Hold Us Back."*

—Carlton Douglas Ridenhour

P.E.A.C.E. Love & Respect to William Jonathan Drayton Jr. aka Flavor Flav, Norman Lee Rogers aka Terminator X, Richard Griffin aka Professor Griff, Lisa Williamson aka Sister Souljah, Hank & Keith Shocklee, and Eric "Vietnam" Sadler aka The Bomb Squad, The S1Ws and all members of the incomparable group PUBLIC ENEMY

Knowledgeable, Powerful; his oratorical abilities unrivaled

Revealed to me the ills of "*Beef*"; instructed me to eat for survival

Single-handedly he candidly handed me knowledge that reigned supreme

Opened the minds of the mentally blind with wisdom that framed my
   inner Being

Naturally he actively promoted Positivity, P.E.A.C.E. and Unity

Educated in the streets, yet his intellect positively influenced me.

   —Lawrence Kris Parker

P.E.A.C.E. Love & Respect to Scott LaRock (Rest In Power)
P.E.A.C.E. Love & Respect to all members of BOOGIE DOWN
PRODUCTIONS aka BDP

Raw Energy sustained in the Essence of a man

Activated every time he rhymed with a mic in his hand

Knowledgeable to the Nth degree; mathematics, science, and history

Irrefutable evidence, will you not agree, bestowed upon us in *"The Mystery"*; a

Masterfully crafted composition; listen, can anyone do it better?

    Eye advise you to let him guide you through *"The 18th Letter."*

    —William Michael Griffin Jr.

    P.E.A.C.E. Love & Respect to Louis Eric Barrier aka Eric B.

P.E.A.C.E. Love & Respect to Michael Small aka Mike Gee, Nathaniel Hall aka Afrika Baby Bam, and Sammy Burwell aka DJ Sammy B, collectively known as The Jungle Brothers

P.E.A.C.E. Love & Respect to Kelvin Mercer aka Posdnuos, David Jolicoeur aka Trugoy (Rest In Power), and Vincent Mason aka Maseo, collectively known as De La Soul

P.E.A.C.E. Love & Respect to Maxwell Dixon aka Grand Puba, Lorenzo Dechalus aka Lord Jamar, and Derek Murphy aka Sadat X, collectively known as Brand Nubian

P.E.A.C.E. Love & Respect to Joseph Simmons aka Run, Darryl McDaniels aka DMC, and Jason Mizell aka Jam Master Jay (Rest In Power), collectively known as Run-DMC

P.E.A.C.E. Love & Respect to Nathaniel Thomas Wilson aka Kool G. Rap and Thomas E. Pough aka DJ Polo

P.E.A.C.E. Love & Respect to Brad Terrence Jordan aka Scarface, William James Dennison aka Willie D, and Richard William Stephen Shaw aka Bushwick Bill (RestIn Power) collectively known as The Geto Boys

P.E.A.C.E. Love & Respect to O'Shea Jackson Sr. aka Ice Cube, Eric Lynn Wright aka Eazy-E (Rest In Power), Lorenzo Jerald Patterson aka MC Ren, Andre Romell Young aka Dr. Dre, Tracy Lynn Curry aka The D.O.C., and Antoine Carraby aka DJ Yella collectively known as NWA

My Journey Into The Light

Submerged in total darkness my 3rd Eye becomes my bond
Between my physical existence of myself; of Life and death beyond
Spiritually enlightened, never frightened of my fate
My destiny shall guide me on a path narrow and straight
Though judgment be reserved, Eye don't deserve to dwell in darkness
So knowledge becomes the nourishment that fills my empty carcass
As Eye begin My Journey; a voice says "Step into The Light"
But The Light it burns me and it takes away my sight
Eye stare into The Light but the glare is just too bright
My body trembles slight then Eye lose my strength to fight
Eye quickly try to flee but my wings won't take to flight
Try as Eye might I've been captured by The Light
Overcome by fright Eye begin to fear The Light
The voice says "Do not worry; You must hurry to The Light
If you just accept The Light, everything shall be alright"
No longer must Eye fight so Eye step into The Light
Embraced by The Light I'm given Love and strength anew
Now The Light becomes My Life because The Light was always You.

Love Thy Self (Ode To Dawn)

When your hopes and dreams seem to have been shattered
When it feels as though you've lost everything that mattered

Love Thy Self

When your hidden fears appear to overcome you completely
When you are no longer with the One you Love so deeply

Love Thy Self

When you endure emotional pain but are too strong to cry
When you strive to regain true Love but are too weak to try

Love Thy Self

When you gave yourself to me hoping I would be your man
My Love for you was true but I didn't understand; Eye must

Love Thy Self

My Beautiful Soul

As Eye gaze upon the array of such Beauty untold
I Am amazed by the display of such Beauty One holds
The design is flawless, all is Beauty to behold
In my mind Eye call this "My Beautiful Soul"
My Beautiful Soul sees the Beauty unfold
Revealed to me only; the Beauty in code
My Beautiful Soul knows the Beauty's unknown
Concealed from all others, the Beauty's my own
My Beautiful Soul touches the Beauty below
And lift up its Spirit so the Beauty can grow
My Beautiful Soul speaks to the beauty in whispers
It dutifully answers; the Beauty's my elixir
The Soul so full of Beauty, the Beauty so full of Soul
In my heart Eye know truly, the truth must be told
Though Beautiful to behold, her Beautiful Soul
May make me lose control, of My Beautiful Soul ...
My Beautiful Soul

Sunday July 10, 2011

Used Tool

I used to feel sorry for myself in droves
I used to feel bad because I had no clothes
I used to feel depressed because I couldn't provide
I used to feel sick because I'd died inside
I used to feel ill because I had no money
I used to feel like laughing but Life was unfunny
I used to feel lost, never ever to be found
I used to feel much better whenever Lillie was around
I used to feel like crying but Eye never shed a tear
I used to feel like dying a little more each year
I used to feel like madness had its hold on my brain
I used to feel sadness, though sadly enough, never pain
I used to feel hatred; I couldn't take it anymore
I used to feel worthless like a purchase in a penny store
I used to feel different as if I didn't belong
I used to feel weak even when Eye was strong
I used to feel repulsive; who would even bear to look at me?!
I used to feel the iniquity that shaped my soul so crookedly
I used to feel defeated Eye needed Jesus in My Life
I used to feel those thoughts from my wife and she was right
I used to feel so lazy; I was definitely going crazy until Eye heard the words spoken by the Lord and they were "Praise Me"
I used to feel foolish now Eye know I was a fool when the O.G. boldly told me the words "used to" means **used** as a **too**l.

Saturday July 16, 2011

Isolated Incidents of Inconsistency

Eye isolate myself from everyone else save myself

It is a skill I've developed and of which I've become quite efficient
As Eye inconclusively state conclusively; I Am consistently inconsistent

The One thing Eye do know is I don't know a thing

A veritable source of useful useless information
My brain cells are magnificent troops imperfect in-formation

Though Eye possess knowledge and through age, attained wisdom;
understanding eludes me

Thus, lack of understanding allows for the potential of
ignorance to envelop me
Therefore, my ways and actions may be those of a fool
even though I think Eye think so intelligently.

I admit to doing shhh... that can be considered not quite right
I Am consistently inconsistent in all but three aspects of My Life

First, the foods that Eye eat are simply the same for weeks and weeks
Secondly, Eye think of the way that Eye Love; I'd say that it's way too deep
Finally, what comes to mind to me is my firm belief in honesty
As a youth Eye pledged allegiance to Truth and do everything
to live Life honestly

Eye promised to be a Man of honesty even though
Eye know promises break

I veered off the path that Eye was shown from the shaft,
that's the last promise I'd ever make

Hence ... I Am consistently inconsistent;
I'm consistently resistant to change

I've been labeled disabled, told I was slow, weird,
even eerie and strange

B.U.T. Eye take no heed to those seeds that are sown
and the shade that is thrown from a distance

Because Eye have known since Eye was grown that
what I Am is consistently inconsistent.

Saturday July 16, 2011

Before Me

What is this written Eye see Before Me?
It's the word before, before I **used to**ol be
<u>My Beautiful Soul</u> wasn't always so attractive
Before GOD took control the devil held me captive
<u>Isolated Incidents of Inconsistency</u> plagued me
I recall being appalled by my behavior, though vaguely
Before I took to my knees and cried Please! GOD save me!
I just looked, shook my head and said These Jesus freaks crazy!
Now that freak is me but I've always been a freak
In every sense of the word but no longer, so to speak
And though I have far to go; <u>As of Yet (Untitled)</u>
Eye have come to know GOD's Love is a Love unrivaled
But so is His wrath so Eye ask myself this ...
Do Eye remain on His path or be cast into the abyss
It's seemingly obvious; I've just got to stay forever focused
Patient in tribulation, strong of Faith, and never hopeless
GOD knows my heart and mind and everything I Am to be
Even before me He restored me so for His glory ... <u>I Am Me</u>.

Wednesday July 20, 2011

Homeless To Heaven

I once self-professed to be blessed to be wise
So as a test I dressed as a homeless man in disguise
I encountered a youth who knew grains of the Truth
Though I knew little more, Eye remained resolute
We bantered about Baal; we jousted about Jesus
We probed the issue of plagues, natural disasters, diseases
From Genesis to Lamentations, to Psalms, Romans, Revelations
We delved deep but failed to agree during our deep conversation
He invited me to share his viewpoint; I respectfully declined
By all means you are welcome to definitely share mine
Which are simple and pure, this I humbly partake of
My Faith and my trust of Jesus; above all, there is Love
Now many seek signs, yet none shall be given
Save to those whom He chose as His One true and living
Sons and daughters; Son, see those waters? Watch closely as they part
For Eye have the Faith of a mustard seed, indeed GOD knows my heart
Yes Lord! Draw your sword! Let your mighty roar be heard!
Let those who hear lend their ear and obey your every word
Let those who see, may they be eternally Blessed by Your Grace
Though we know your invisible attributes to be absolute,
today may we know your face
Without delay the once sunny day became ominous, gloomy and grey
Lightning crackled, thunder hackled the land and bodies of water began to sway
Back and forth, to and fro, it looked as though the liquid parted
Then everything suddenly ceased just as quickly as it started
Yet there upon the sky O'Lord boomed a luminous Heavenly vision
Thy Kingdom come, thy will be done, "My son are you ready to make a decision?"
He said to me, "Yeah everything you said and showed me was pretty cool
But you see, to me you'll always be, just a homeless old pitiful Fool."

Monday July 25, 2011

Rarely Am I

I Am soft-spoken, rarely Am I heard
My thoughts are not open, Eye rarely speak a word
I Am heartbroken, rarely does Love last for me
My Spirit is not the purest, but Eye rarely commit blasphemy
I Am arms open, rarely is anyone rejected
My generosity is possibly why I Am rarely disrespected
I Am withdrawn within my shell; rarely do you see me truly
My appearance is not adherent to those who supposedly define Beauty;
yet I Am Beautiful to those who truly know Beauty in its rarest form
My ethereal Being beneath what you're seeing is
truly the Beauty-fullest Being born.

Sunday November 02, 2014

As Eye Am

Eye traveled the World many times in my mind
Eye took the name World to bring P.E.A.C.E. to mankind
And womankind alike, to find a Woman Eye could like
Because Eye Love everyone B.U.T. no One is my type
I'm a Bridger of Light with a dark heart complexion
GAIA giver of Life; she sparked my connection
Look upon my face; that's what you see first
It's not a pretty sight; my insides seem worse
Years of frustration seething within; encompassed by chaos, breathing in sin
Heart full of hate; anger courses through my veins
My atria aches; dangerous impulses pulsate through my brain
Heart full of Love; Eye give of myself freely
My ventricles are virginal; but that's not how you see me
To see me as you see me is merely a facade
What is truly to be seen is between me and my GOD
My GOD is Pure Energy, the Essence of All
Inner-G of Divinity and Blessings to all
Eye don't profess to know the lessons because I Am not of the Nation
But Eye got knowledge of self due to self-manifestation
My education's of alleys and avenues mixed with scholastic abilities
Indoctrinated in the streets, classroom seats, and correctional facilities
Always profound; Eye keep an earthbound foundation
Representing for the 4 billion 400 million of our Nation
Being beneficent I'm symbolic to the Sun
Understanding is the seed that you breed as my Wisdom.

Thursday March 06, 2008
Monday January 01, 2018

Firm In My Faith

I stand firm in my faith; Eye shall not waver
Eye Love Myself; I Love thy neighbor
My Love of GOD is second to none
Test my resolve, you get seconds to run
GOD is for me so no One's against me
Romans 8:31 Sun convinced me
GOD got me; my motto, my creed
GOD got me; now follow my lead
I Am Being Enlightened
Lesser beings would be frightened
B.U.T. my Inner-G is heightened
So Eye stand tall as a Titan
Wait ... I misspoke; not enlightened B.U.T. reminded
Ienindra removed the yoke so Eye know I Am no longer blinded
If it's P.E.A.C.E. that Eye seek, it's the P.E.A.C.E. of me that's been hidden
Which won't be exposed if my 3rd Eye closed, so Eye
Pray to GAIA give me vision
In that instance in the distance Eye sensed dimensions in descension
Which prompted me to promptly mention the existence of Ascension
To any and all who'll listen; pay attention; heed the signs
To become a collective is the objective; One Body, One
Soul, One Spirit, One Heart, One Mind.

B.U.T. (Born Universal Truth)
P.E.A.C.E. (Positive Energy Activates Continuous Enlightment)

Land of the Thief / **Home of the Slave**

We Originals need to go back to those days when those snakes
couldn't take us away and then trade us ...

Eye worship no devil, no false idol, hell no; in my Temple
Eye resemble the great GOD who made us ...

Birthed from the womb of a Woman of Beauty; my intellect says
respect and protect; it's my duty ...

To revive eighty-five uncivilized beasts; priests speak of P.E.A.C.E.
as Eye rise from the East ...

The degrees of my knowledge become latitude; time zones separate,
then the snakes are subdued ...

Captured the grafted with mind-crafted tactics; calculate their fate
with great Black mathematics ...

Teach to Brianna to honor thy Father and Mother of Earth; B.U.T. first;
learn the legacy of her birth ...

08/10/94 like 1894; the year sinners feared retribution; solution;
Revolution and War ...

My blood sweat and tears are what covers my grave;
in the Land of the Thief / **Home of the Slave**

A (Womb)an's Wealth

Respect her for what she's worth
If you were able to give birth
Would you treat a woman worse
Than you already treat her
Pretending not to need her

Understand you came from a woman (Whoa man)
Go slow man, because no man

Has the right; to raise his hands to a woman in any type of fight

Use your mental might, or your mental might misguide you

By calling her a bitch; is that really the bitch inside you?

If so, why lie to yourself and why lie to everyone else?

You need to go back to the Essence and explore the depths of
<u>A (Womb)an's Wealth</u>.

Tuesday March 08, 2011
International Women's Day

A Father's Foundation

The duty of a Father is to <u>Fat her</u> with knowledge

To provide her with the best possible Life, just as GOD did

A Father encourages his daughter to exceed her limitations

He nourishes her to succeed, yet harbors no expectations

A Father offers support, unconditional Love, and consideration

A Woman's true worth is embedded deep within the Earth
Encompassed by <u>A Father's Foundation</u>.

Though Eye have none, same applies to a son,
for Fathers who raise boys to men.

Sunday June 19, 2011
Father's Day

Intercorrectional Correspondence

Iz, Let me enlighten you ...

Da game ain't da same without you as my coach.
I'm still the top-ranked playa so guess who Eye wrote.
My ex and yes, I'm still tryin' to get at dat Princess.
Once I get her address, I'mma bless her with my mental fitness;
And see what transpires, I'mma try her; see where her head's at;
If ain't nothin' hapn'n, then fuck it; I'mma dead dat.
B.U.T. on anotha level here's some shhh... 4u2 swallow;
I caught a tier II; they'll probably serve me tomorrow.
For some str8 bullshhh... destruction of State Property;
But I'mma try to beat it bcuz it wasn't written properly.
But you know how they pump in this chump ass spot;
Even when you in the right, in their eyes, you're not.
And peep this shhh...; Sha might be there in Bare Hill wit you;
Bcuz he threw hands wit Panama; the dude who used to be on my crew.
The funnystyle cat that moved down to the dog pound;
Anyway, they went at it, now neither one of them's around.
I Pray you stay strong to take on what Life may bring;
Physically fit, mentally swift, and emotionally equipped to deal with anything.

Just because I'm away from you doesn't mean I'm astray from you

And because I'm a man that's true to myself, I feel that I must say to you

Stop! Taking my heart and breaking my heart and making my heart feel pain; because

Once my heart is totally torn apart, it will never heal the same

Now you can decide to stay by my side and abide by Jason's rule

Make no mistake; I'll give, you can take, but don't play me for a fool

I'd die for you Babygirl, but to live for you is better

Some say "Jay, she put you through too much; Yo how the fuck you let her?"

That's when they begin to stream down my face like a flood

It's my misty tears for Misti that swiftly turn from tears to blood.

Vesuvius once rose as a strong, mighty mountain

Athena, as lore goes, bathed in a gore blood-filled fountain

Sirens are said to have led sailors wayward, singing songs of rapture

Hades, so say sages, was plagued by Spirits who sought Heaven to capture

The most majestic of all, in these tall tales told, was none other than Zeus

Every thought of his became reality, according to the fantasy,

    thus their Universe was produced

Even though you may not fathom the magnitude of all of this

    We should all comprehend; in the end, it's mostly Myth(?)

Can it be possible? Am Eye to believe what my eyes are seeing?

An angel dwells amongst us in the form of a human being

Righteous in the name of thy Lord, her faith is strong and shall never waver

Mighty is your word, O' Lord; she embraces you as her Savior

Even in times of darkness, His Light is there to guide her

Now His Light becomes the source of Life embedded deep inside her.

*

Justice seekers scream fiercely for freedom from oppression

Underdeveloped nations dream of absolution and invocation of Blessings

Land, air, and sea are the dominions to be dominated

Israel and Palestine, though carefully contemplated,

    shouldn't be so complicated

And through it all, America stands so tall, high and mighty,

    never wavering or faltering

    Yet look how many lives our lifestyles are altering.

Recently our society has been cast into confusion

Our country is at war with itself with no imminent conclusion

Solutions are sought, yet nothing has been solved

Evolution created a wiser, gentler human; yet who of us have actually evolved

Moreover, with the war over, there'd be no room for political conjecture

Also there'd be no place to "liberate" for America,

    the Great Democracy Protector

Reading this, you may insist that I Am simply anti-American; but

You'd be wrong; my Love of country strong, though

    Eye can't quite agree we the paragon; of Truth, Justice, and Virtue.

The Truth, so I've heard, shall set you free

Even though it's merely a word, its power is dear to me

Someone once told me, "There is never a need to lie"

So Eye adhered to those words closely and forever agreed to try,

    to never speak a lie

And though there are moments in Life when deception seems warranted

    or tolerable

You must rise above the lies to show that you are indeed,

    more knowledgeable

Everyone has a fate they must face in their Life

    So live yours full of Truth because a lie can never be right.

Be patient; GOD is with you. Be yourself; you are beautiful;

    be strong; all will be fine

Even when the darkness descends, the Light will eventually shine

Think positive thoughts; think purely; think of positive results;

    Life will surely be better

Hopefully you will become empowered with strength

    in the form of this letter

Zaida you provide a smile full of warmth, complete compassion

And not to be a man of blasphemy, so GOD, please forgive me for asking

Is this possibly the way you properly pay the angels

    who perform your work?

Desperately Eye Pray that You mercifully take away all her pain,

    frustration, and hurt

And replace her angst with a Heavenly "Thanks"

    Which allows her to know her true worth.

Intelligence is required through years of training and understanding

Divinity defines you intricately; patient and undemanding

As always, in all ways, you amaze us with your grace; the

Radiance of your beauty soothes me like a warm embrace

Majestic, like the Queen you were bred to be

Making your acquaintance has motivated me professionally

You have truly inspired me to reveal the best in me

Some may speculate that it was fate, yet Eye know it to be destiny.

*

Eternal youth and everlasting Life; exists for the righteous, but at what price

Dedicate yourself to the most beneficent

In all of Its glory, It's truly omnipotent

Thrive to divide from the immoral ways of the wicked

Heed to righteousness and you might just receive your ticket.

Realistically speaking, you are the epitome

Of what, supposedly, a real man is supposed to be

Beliefs that you adhere to endears me to you

Even in the midst of iniquity, you remain righteous and true

Resounding in your faith; steadfast, never bending

Though the journey to eternal happiness is a path that has no ending

Only you, by the Grace of GOD, shall truly live your Life

    Yet it is only the Grace of GOD, whom shall judge what is right.

Definitely deserving

Ever serving

Lord's One

GOD's Son

Ascension attained

Divinely

Ordained

OUTER LIMITS

Please do not attempt to refute what Eye display
Because I Am firm in my Faith and Eye believe what Eye say
Eye Pray every day and every day Eye receive my Blessings
While you refuse to see the Truth and go through Life guessing
My GOD is my Savior; my Savior's My Energy
I've been delivered from slave labor because Eye Minister My Inner-G
In me this image, every blemish, every crevice, every line
Was crafted in Its image through the presence of time
Time being conceptual with perpetual parameters
It was Tesla who tested time with machines designed for future planeters
Or planeteers with plans for spheres scattered throughout outer atmospheres
Orbs orbiting everything and no thing in unison;
ordering the hoarding and boarding of UFOs to enclose humans in.

My Plight, My Descent, My Fight, Against ...

My descent into madness gradually commences
Eye can't formulate a thought into a sensible sentence
My decision-making process has become contaminated
Eye need protection from my thoughts, I need my brain laminated
You wouldn't believe the tricks my mind keep on playing
My memory's shot to shhh... what the ... what was Eye jest saying?
Anytime Eye contemplate Eye find it hard to concentrate
My mind is in a constant state, of darkness; Death may have to wait
Thus Eye Wait
For a voice to speak to me; Eye seek the P.E.A.C.E.; I Am looking for the Light
But all Eye see is darkness so I sit in the dark and start to write
My plight isn't uncommon; I'm in the same shituation
As over half the population in this overpopulous Nation
I'm facing bankruptcy, poverty, practically extinction
No saving me through Snag-a-job, Indeed, Monster, or LinkedIn
I'm thinking "How the fluck did it ever get so bad?"
I'm thinking "Why the fluck don't Brianna know her Dad?"
But honestly it's probably for the best because I'm a mess
And the more she knows about me, the less she'll be impressed
More or less my moral-less compass is pointing south
Due to my dubious actions and the words emerged from my mouth
My plight; my descent represents a scintilla of sorrow or sadness
Because the depths of my descent are evident in my fight against my madness.

wasted

Damn; another day gone by ... wasted
Greatness comes once in a Lifetime ... embrace it
Many of these writers write alike ... basic
You readers need to open up your eyes ... lasik
And cease being spoon-fed drivel ... taste it
Time to put foot to the mediocre middle ... place kick
All you internet intellects on Facebook ... face it
All you "killers" and "hitters" on Insta and Twitter ... erase it
Taking swings at minor things, playing it safe ... base hit
Eye profess to be the best; took the test and yes, Eye ... aced it

So

To those who have transgressed against me; apology accepted
GOoD fate to you in the future and stay well protected
I expected no less from those of low intellect
Yet Eye still carry myself with the utmost respect
Up close let's inspect and analyze Mr. P.E.A.C.E.
Eye remained at peace even before the lies ceased
Even before the remains of the name Howard died, deceased
Eye came to refute charges with my sharkskin suit sharply creased
Even though the judge refused to budge in my case
Eye hold no grudge against those who fall from grace
Or those who are misguided, hiding in the shadows preparing to pounce
But remember this before I bounce; it's the man who counts
the money, not the money the man counts that counts;
because
Manners will take you where money won't.

Young 'un On the Run!

Once upon a time not long ago, when people stayed fitted and kept that dough
Where po-po was corrupt and ran the whole city
One young 'un went nuts and started to git gritty
(He said) "I'm sick of being broke, down low as the dirt"
Grabbed the pistol grip pump jumped up to work
Hit the check cashing spot at the end of the block
Backing out the door, he let off a quick shot
Laid everybody down in a house on Breeze and Third
Came out with a come-up, three gees and a bird
Gave the powder to the wildest young 'uns on the block
But little did he know one of the kids was a cop
Undercovers tried to smother the brother; he wasn't having it
Grabbed the artillery out of Aunt Lillie's cabinet
Hit the fire escape to make his way to his Impala
Cop let off a shot, he shot back, the cop hollered
"Officer down! officer down!" the airwaves were alit
Kid started up the whip, hit the gas, then he split
Raced up the block, cops hot in pursuit
Police shout out the PA system "Stop or I'll shoot"!
He tried to execute a right turn doing eighty
Clipped a whip, flipped the whip, and landed on an old lady
Crawled out the wreck, bruised and battered but not broken
Sprawled on the ground, face down, car smoking
'Trol roll up, jump out 'bout twenty deep
Surround the grid while the kid struggle to get to his feet
Weak as can be he still reach for his heat
The cops pop off 80 shots, four apiece for each
All said and done the young 'un never had hope
It's a tragedy and bad as it be, it's not a joke
So to all the Lost Souls in this city of strife
Find a way to find your way that one day may save your Life.

P.E.A.C.E. Love & Respect to Richard Martin Lloyd Walters
aka Slick Rick and Douglas Davis aka Doug E. Fresh

I Was Never Not Aware That Eye Would Be Awakened

(Lion's Gate 08/08/2019 - Treasure Island, Florida)

She came from another planet; it seemed like it was lunacy
I didn't take it for granted; Eye seized the opportunity
She was commissioned for a mission to restore the balance
I was reconditioned to ignore the challenge
B.U.T. Eye was preconditioned to accept her words
Her philosophy on Life was the best Eye heard
I've always been a firm believer; never ever a skeptic
B.U.T. don't feed me bullshhh... and expect me to just accept it
Plus, no matter what, Eye trust my instincts instinctively
And I never truly cared what people do or do not think of me
Yet in Ienindra's case this was primarily not the case
As we sat at the cafe table sharing our space face to face
She regaled me with a tale of thee most fascinating proportions
How Eye was a Bridger of Light tasked with balancing distortion
How RahYin, her visiting friend, was actually her adversary
In a Battle of Beings being engaged on Earth and interplanetary
How after being submerged, she emerged from the water crystalline, glistening
Eye witnessed her glitches she freely showed us and
everything she told us, Eye took heed and Eye was listening.

MY EVERY LIVIN' FANTASY

She's beautiful and I Am jest too old
She's a Lovely girl in my ugly World
She's fasscinating and I'm fascinated
She's captivating and I'm captivated
She pushed my button now I'm activated
Eye was GOoD with nothing now I'm motivated ...

It seems to me; you're like my every livin' fantasy
Can't get you out my mind though Eye been tryin,' girl you're killin' me
Want you to forever be mine all of the time, I mean habitually
Sittin' here drunk on this wine, drunk out my mind and it's a bitch to see me
Wastin' all of my time tryin' to find the words to say to you
Thought I made it glass when the reverend asked me to say I do
So much time has passed, so far in our past, or is it deja vu
Eye know we can make this last, or is this the last, day I lay with you
Tell me how we can get past this, what must I do just to stay with you
If worse comes to worst, I'll go to church and even Pray with you.

You're My / I'm Your Pain

You're taking away ... Everything that means anything to me
Stop, look what you're doing, listen to your Family
Your Mama said I'm the Man for you and even your Daddy agree
Whatever you choose to do don't do just because you're mad at me
I may have lied to you just a few times in the past but I never slept around
Even gave you two of the best numbers I had and baby the rest you found
You put me in hot water for a week real deep but you would not let me drown
Hold up, wait a minute, let me speak, I'll be brief; I promise I won't let you down
I'll cook, I'll clean; do all the type of things that I never did before
Whatever it takes I'll make up for my mistakes; I promise I'll give you more ...

You're my pain ... Where's my strength and pride? It's a shame
Because I'm empty inside. I'm just trying to find myself ... for myself.

I'm your pain ... Where's your Love and worth? It's a shame
Because this Love it hurts. How much Love will it take to work this out? ...
Can we work this out?

Do Eye detect a tinge of sadness behind those Lovely eyes of yours

Are your tears the type to come at night like when it rains it pours

Maybe not as severe as a shower but Damaris I'm here to empower

All you have to do is allow me to; all I need is maybe an hour

Reaching out to you with arms extended to pull you into my chest

I've come to you to comfort you and do more, but never less

Seems sudden but if we do nothing to further the fervor we started

Potentially, for HSPs like you and me,

    could lead us both to be broken-hearted.

Deep unto you yet Eye always want deeper

As far as Eye can get but I can't seem to reach her

My Mother's a Saint; her Father's a Preacher

And both of us know that GOD is an Ether-

Real Entity; eventually we'll become One

I won't cease to please her until she be-comes

She's given me her Light; her mind and her Energy

      EYE

Pray that she'll stay and be mine til Infinity

Every essence of her presence I've beholden is golden

Regardless of my hardness, it's me she has chosen

Even when she's closed in, she opens up to accept me

Zealously, the pleasure she receives cannot be achieved through anyone

    except me.

Wednesday August 09, 2017

Eye Dream of Damaris

Eye dream of Damaris like Major Nelson "*Dream of Jeannie*"
She didn't want to share this but she felt something when she seen me
Maybe she was a little embarrassed because she knew she made me nervous
But little did she foresee that Eye would forever be at her service
She never anticipated for us to have such "*Good Times*" together
GOoD and golden for me, but she could possibly do better (not exxxact-Lee)
My expectations of us lasting was low because
she was so full of grace, elegance, and style
So beautifully built equipped; she "*Bewitched*" me with her smile
"*What's Happening*" to me? I'm "Re-run"ning the scene
of how we first met in my head
Eye saw her at the light, leaving "*The Office*" of ORMC,
and this is what she said ...

Actually, it jest occurred to me; it's a blur to me what was spoken
Because while my eyes, ears, mouth, and mind were closed;
my heart was the only part open.

Wednesday August 09, 2017

Every Ballad Ever Written

Every ballad ever written is an invalid description, not an
actual depiction, of the Love Eye feel for You
If I was never bitten by the Love bug in your "kitchen,"
I wouldn't be on this *Mission of Love*; you feel it too
Eye crave my daily dosage, lick the "stamp" and pay the
postage, I'm the host and you're my hostess, RSVP if your free-key
Will unlock the One lock closest, to the One spot Eye want
most it's, above your belly below your shoulders;
the part of me I give to you free-Lee so answer me this ...

Where do you disappear to when you drift away from me?
Are you alone in your lonely zone? Is it a place you prefer to be?
How do you refer to me when you speak of me in your mind?
When will you return to me to pursue the P.E.A.C.E. we seek to find?
When I seek conversation why do you cease communication?
When I attempt unification why do you revoke my invitation?
Has our interactions of late been to your satisfaction enough to sate?
What more must it take for us to just embrace, what began for
us as lust, evolved to Trust and Love and Fate?

PLEASE BE ADVISED:

The following poems that are featured in the remainder of this book contain graphic and explicit words and/or phrases that may elicit thoughts of a sexual nature. If you are considered to be or deemed to be, by yourself or anyone else, easily offended sexually or a relatively prudish person, please refrain from further perusing of the impending musings. If not, please enjoy the joy of the prose Eye present.

YOU HAVE BEEN ADVISED

Introduction To ...

I got too **deep** into you just like Eye always do
I guess Eye always knew it was just too GOoD to be true
But you didn't have to guess; you already knew what we'd become
How I'd crave you and become a slave to you and you'd run and leave me numb
I was being dumb for trying to blindly make you mine
I should have relented when you attempted to end it the second time
But I pretended that it was fine with delusions of Damaris in my mind
Knowing after that time we'd never reach Chapter 69

*

(Chapped Her 69)

As Eye cum to the conclusion of my titillating tales to you
The illusion of Beauty in my mind still pales to you
Eye attempted to find in you what others have failed to do
Which is now exempt because I now have failed to do too
Although Eye can still smell you and taste you in my dreams
Eye can feel you on my face and savor the taste of your pastry cream
I digress ... I'm repressed; sexually it's been consecutively 8 weeks
Since we've seen each other, since I've been your Lover
with my face between your cheeks
And you know that's a place Eye Love; I call it my comfort zone
Me beneath, you sitting above; I've cum to make you moan.

my unbridled everlasting passion eXXXploads

Lissandra was knock-kneed, pigeon-toed, and bow-legged
I hit her with my dick like a fist so she called me knuckle-headed
I took to calling her Luscious because I wood bust quick every time
Then I wood interrogate that pussy for hours and never drop a dime
After dark in Genessee Valley Park in the backseat of my Chevy
She got ready to greet my meat and we got heated, hot and heavy
Pounding at a resounding pace, I was pumping too fast
I slipped out, she gripped the stout and put it plump in her ass.

*

Pumpkin was sumthin of a cougar before the word was in fashion
She was 36 doing tricks on my dick; I was 18 and Pumpkin smashin'
I called her Pumpkin Pussykin 'cause she could spin, clutch and squeeze
She called me Drill Sergeant for how I made her bend and touch her knees
We fucked for 8 weeks straight til her man got released,
From prison so her decision was our tryst had to cease.

*

Tisheka was a freak of a completely different stature
She asked me if she fell for me would I be there to catch her
And without hesitation I told Sheka I had her
She had a "man at home" situation and it didn't even matter
6'2 in her "hooker boots" she had me looking like a midget
What I lacked in height I made up for the length of my digit
She didn't care, we did it anywhere; in private or public
No inhibitions, any position, the more risque I'd say, the more that she Loved it.

*

I applaud Maude because that broad saved my fuck'n Life
She came to me in my time of need; not just once butt fuck'n twice
Keuka Lake I resigned my fate and sunk to the bottom
Eye prayed with grace, saw her face, and heard her say "I got him"
That night I almost died Eye planted a seed inside of Maude
She was feeling me but she revealed to me she wasn't ready so she made "that call"
Through it all she and I didn't all ways see Eye to Eye
B.U.T. her mentality matched her sexuality; A-One bonafide.

*

Eye hear Dawn, dear Dawn; how long have you been gone?
Not quite long enough, she might have had some of the strongest stuff
I was wrong for her; she was rite for me;
Sometimes Eye reflect on how our Life could be
What could have been or should have been would have been we be together
But instead of sharing my bed she became my Friend For Life (FFL) forever.

*

And then of course there's Menda who I never should have surrendered
We started off so tender, then got ferocious for most of November, '93 see ...
It all began in 1989, when we met at Edison Tech, Eye thought "Damn she so fine"
And she liked my rep so I stepped to her to pursue her,
In the dean's office talking to the secretary, Gloria, who knew her
Eye thought she was in trouble; she had a knack for that
so that's the assumption I made
But for once in many months she was being a "good girl"
working as a dean's aide

We flirted then I blurted "Men, I'll probably hit it, stick around
for a minute, then straight up quit it"
She said "Will if I give you the P you'll be like, look'n for me
in the daytime with a bright flashlight"
So we booked up and we hooked up every day of the week
Either I was at her house or she was under my sheets
Until it ended in December, but damn I'll always remember
How she kept both my heads whirling like Eye was twirling in a blender
She was One of my greatest Lovers butt that's not what makes me Love her
The fact that's most vital, she bears the title of Brianna's Mother.

*

Bree oh Bree; where would I be without Bree Marie
So shy, so petite, such a pure sweet treat to eat
That demure demeanor disguised a surprise beast in bed
That might be a slight embellishment I tell myself at least in my head
More to the point she was submissive and permissive of me putting in work
She was timid butt nothing was off limits, I could go anywhere; put it in; insert
She did this "trick" she called 'the bricks' where she'd flex her quad muscles
That shhh... got me so aroused, so endowed I be-came renamed
Mr. Quick to Bust bro.

*

Brittany V, she was abs-so-loot-Lee, certainly a vision to see
Easy decision for me to fluck with Brittany V
One of the five "baddest bitches" in Da R-O-C
Wit an azz dat phat shhh... I gotta eat, beat, repeat
We went at it like some rabbits for about six weeks

Like addicts wit da habits of habitual freaks
Oh my GOD it was so erotic so Eye called her my GODdess
In all my years of existence my dick has never been as hard as,
GODdess got it, so GOD got me the Angel that Eye needed
So Eye thanked Him every time from every angle Eye beat it.

*

Dear Damaris, allow me to share this; I'm not embarrassed to say
Eye miss you and it's got me feeling some type of way
Eye miss you, "Lil Me," a bit more than Eye care to admit
Eye miss you and missing you sure do stink like shhh...
Eye miss your Beauty and your booty and your cooty I licked
Eye miss being well around you; well around you Eye wasn't ever sick
Eye miss you and how your Inner-G is in perfect symmetry to mine
Eye miss you for your body, heart, soul, Spirit and mind
Eye miss how we'd meet in a discreet, secret location
Eye miss how you'd make me wait to taste you then break through, penetration
Eye miss the way we kiss full of bliss and so erotic
Eye miss the essence of your presence so effervescent and exotic.

Me & Mr. Death (1992)
(The Saga Continues)

I encountered Mr. Death in the murky depths of Keuka Lake
Even as the water churned Eye could discern his putrid face
Eye was in duress due to a drunken, stupid mistake
Resigned to my fate, Eye made no attempt at a futile escape
Yet, let me take you back mere moments before that when I sat on a dock
Finishing a rapidly diminishing 40-ounce bottle of Private Stock
It's One o'clock in the a.m. pitch black and I'm sway'n back and forth
Contemplating to continue waiting for Maude to rejoin me
or swim back to the other shore
Where four other couples convened approximately 100 yards away
Why and how I did what I did that day is still slightly somewhat hard to say
I dove in to begin what I thought was a swim towards the aforementioned shore
After 100 yards plus, Eye looked up confusedly, and still swam more
Just then realization set in; struck me, "FUCK ME", it's all gone wrong
I tried to swim back the way I came but I couldn't stay strong
Not long after came complete disaster; Death appeared and he jeered
"Who's your Master?"
My body grew heavy like lead weight, dead weight; I yelled out
"You bastard!" and hoped to stroke faster
But he yoked me by the throat, choked me out and dragged me down
As I fought all Eye thought was "I'm a city nikka, what da
fuck I'm do'n in dis country town 'bout to drown?!"
I wrenched myself free from Death's grip and shot up to the surface
Gasping for air, I screamed "Maude! Maude!" with urgency and purpose
My respite didn't quite last as long as I'd like; Death dunked me again
and we continued our fight
The second time around he kept me down even longer
Eye grew weaker as we plummeted deeper and Mr. Death just got stronger

Not 100% spent, I used my remaining strength to repel Death's attack
I bit and I kicked, swung my elbows and fist, did my all to
resist and get this bitch off my back
He cackled as we grappled, admonishing me sonically with
a screech that I was certain would leave my ears hurtin'
Work'n overtime I threw him over my shoulder; propelled
myself upward, broke the surface and water started spurt'n
Outta my mouth, I shout "Maude! Maude!" in a surprisingly
strong voice, though my limbs are like linguini
Hoping she can hear me 'cause Eye know she cannot see me
It's just too dark, even with the spark of light from the few
flashlights and lanterns held by random people gathering
Alerted to the sounds of me drowning; the commotion
couldn't go unnoticed, nor my panic
On the brink of extinction Eye made the distinction to
relinquish my thinking and began sinking like the *Titanic*
Resigned to my fate, I could not escape, so I sank and sank and sank
Mr. Death reappeared looking solemn, yet severe, and
whispered in my ear "You have but yourself to thank"
He shuttered my eyes and uttered a wise incantation of
reincarnation designed to reassign my soul for him to control
Prepared to let go, Eye ebb and Eye flow, my body burns
cold, but lo and behold, something grabs ahold
Something other than Death; I suddenly recover my breath
Because Maude dove below and returned me to the surface
Though she could not see, she had been rigorously racing to me, or rather
my voice, so my shouts without a doubt, were certainly worth it
Except, I Am imperfect and in my frenzied state of mind
I aggressively grabbed Maude and pulled her down with
me for her first, and my fourth, time
Well, she kept her cool; she was calm under pressure
Her reaction was exactly what we needed; GOD Bless Her

She pulled us back up and swiftly snuffed me in my face
For those who may not know, allow me to rephrase
Maude punched me in my jaw and yelled "STOP! You're gonna kill us both"
That was enough to "wake me up" and make me clutch Maude close
She continued by saying "I got you. I got you. Hold on to me"
Unbeknownst to us, which we could not first see, one of our
companions rowed a canoe to where we would be
Juan operated the oar with the skill and ease of an Olympic athlete
Not much longer after Maude saved me, Juan was there
with the canoe to make the rescue complete
That night I nearly lost My Life Eye planted my seed inside
of Maude, as Mr. Death lurked in the shadows of the corner
I stopped mid-stroke, I start to choke, unhand her ass and
ask "Maude can you see him in the corner"? Butt before
she could focus, POOF, hocus pocus he was gone; Eye tried to warn her.

Me & Mr. Death (2015)

(The Saga Continues)

I was admitted to RGH with a case of ... hmmm ...
let's jest say it was undetermined
Though Eye showed no worries or doubt, the doctors
and Nurses scurried about rather concerned in ...
Asking "Are you having trouble breathing? Can you swallow correctly?"
Eye replied "Looks are deceiving. It really doesn't affect me"
But let me go back to the beginning and explain somewhat in depth
That night full of sinning which brought about my
impending encounter with Mr. Death

*

Eye met a brunette named Jessica Soble
We got drunk together; we never got sober
We went to my place that I once shared with my ex
We defaced the bedroom carpet with all types of sex
For hours on end we devoured each other
She wasn't my friend, Eye wasn't her Love-her
Butt we clicked and I licked her intimates intricately for one hour straight
That may seem a bit much butt trust, it's not the longest Eye ate
Anyway as midday faded away to nightfall
She mounted me and a pronounced imagery was cast upon the rite wall
The image is my nemesis, Mr. Death, yet he's different
Beautiful, luminescent, radiating, magnificent
He's even disguised his evilish vibe
I'm seduced by his new suit but this new form cannot hide

The Truth of who this whoa-man was; a tool to be used against me
I've always been Strong of Heart, yet weak of flesh,
and she was definitely tempting
Eye broke their spell, Eye bid her farewell, and we went our separate way
Three days after somewhat of a disaster occurred
and Eye could be heard to Pray ...
The "disaster" that struck me, some call unlucky, or some
facetiously say was jest genius
My throat and tongue swell to the size of a cowbell,
"semenly" from the 69 minutes of cunnilingus
Have you ever seen any tv episode where the bullfrog creek
toad expands his throat to the fullest?
Well if you have, apparently that image you see was meant
to be me on day three of Mr. Death's Kill List
Thus ... Eye sought Spiritual guidance through Prayer and
was guided to where Eye should be treated to where
Death would be defeated
The *HUGE* lump in my throat was never quite diagnosed
but they injected a collection of drugs intravenously
Regardless of what the doctors instructed, that lump
wasn't to be flucked with, there was no healing me seemingly
On my second night of admission Eye had a premonition,
or rather a vision of Death
Wearing filthy, tattered scrubs, he held a scalpel to my
throat, and made an incision as he sat on my chest
I awoke startled, got up and gargled a sodium saline solution
I returned to the bed and cleared my head of that dreadful Deathly intrusion
After that my slumber is wonderful; Eye sleep solidly
and soundly through the night
Upon arising I Am greeted with a surprisingly delightful sight

The lump is gone! No swelling, no discomfort, it's as if it never happened
But placed upon my lap is this morning's newspaper with the following caption
"Man slain in motel room, two suspects in custody" with a blurry photo of a
man and woman, handcuffed, standing next to a *Toyota Cressida*
Though no one would believe, or even conceive, what was
clear to me, Eye could clearly see that the man and woman
was Mr. Death and his demon temptress Jessica.
What further fueled my fury and consternation
to my already heavy, weary mind
Was strictly because the victim, he was, a friend and a co-worker of mine.

(Rest In Power - Jehon 'Albaniac' Gervalla)

www.ingramcontent.com/pod-product-compliance
Lightning Source LLC
LaVergne TN
LVHW041649060526
838200LV00040B/1775